curiousabout

HOBBY ROBOTS

T0023825

BY LELA NARGI

AMICUS LEARNING

What are you

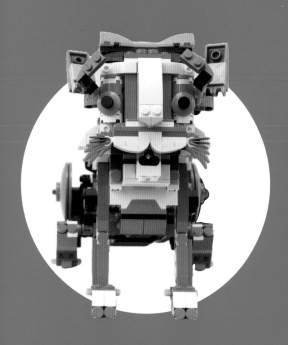

are you

curious about?

CHAPTER THREE

Robots Old and New

PAGE

16

Curious about is published by
Amicus Learning, an imprint of Amicus
P.O. Box 227
Mankato, MN 56002
www.amicuspublishing.us

Editor: Rebecca Glaser
Series and Book Designer: Kathleen Petelinsek
Photo researcher: Omay Ayres

Library of Congress Cataloging-in-Publication Data
Names: Nargi, Lela, author.
Title: Curious about hobby robots / by Lela Nargi.
Description: Mankato, MN : Amicus Learning, an imprint of
Amicus, 2024. | Series: Curious about robotics | Includes
bibliographical references and index. | Audience: Ages 5–9 |
Audience: Grades 2–3 | Summary: "Questions and answers give
kids an understanding about the technology of hobby robots,
including robots built for competitions and robots built just
for fun. Includes infographics to support visual learning and back
matter to support research skills, plus a glossary
and index"—Provided by publisher.
Identifiers: LCCN 2023013337 (print) | LCCN 2023013338
(ebook) | ISBN 9781645496519 (library binding) | ISBN
9781681529400 (paperback) | ISBN 9781645496779 (pdf)
Subjects: LCSH: Robots—Juvenile literature.
| Robotics—Juvenile literature.
Classification: LCC TJ211.2 .N37532 2024 (print) | LCC
TJ211.2 (ebook) | DDC 629.8/92–dc23/eng/20230330
LC record available at https://lccn.loc.gov/2023013337
LC ebook record available at https://lccn.loc.gov/2023013338

Photo credits: Alamy/ukartpics, 16, 17; BMG Solutions/
BMG Solutions, 17; Dreamstime/Dana Rothstein /3,16;
Fandomwiki/Robogames Wiki, 15; iStock/loonger, 19;
Shutterstock/AlesiaKan, 2, 6, 7, arda savasciogullari, 11,
Gargantiopa, cover, ILIA BLIZNYUK, 10, Inside Creative
House, 11, Jacky Co, 22–23, MAB32, 11, Martynova Anna,
8, 9, mijatmijatovic, 11, Min Jing, 13, mohamad firdaus
bin ramli, 14–15, Monkey Business Images, 4, 5, Olena
Yakobchuk, 20–21, Pushy zver, 11, Sorapop Udomsri, 2,12

Printed in China

Are any robots just for fun?

Yes! That's what hobby robots are all about. Kids and adults build these machines. They may be **rovers** that explore. They may be bugs that crawl or race. Maybe they are made to wrestle. Want to hear a joke? Ask a robot.

Robot cars are fun to build with friends.

How can I make robots?

Some robots come in kits. You build them with LEGO sets. When you're done you get a cat that purrs or a dragon that stomps. But you can make them from anything. Try popsicle sticks and googly eyes for the body. Add wheels and a motor to make it move.

You can use old parts to build a robot.

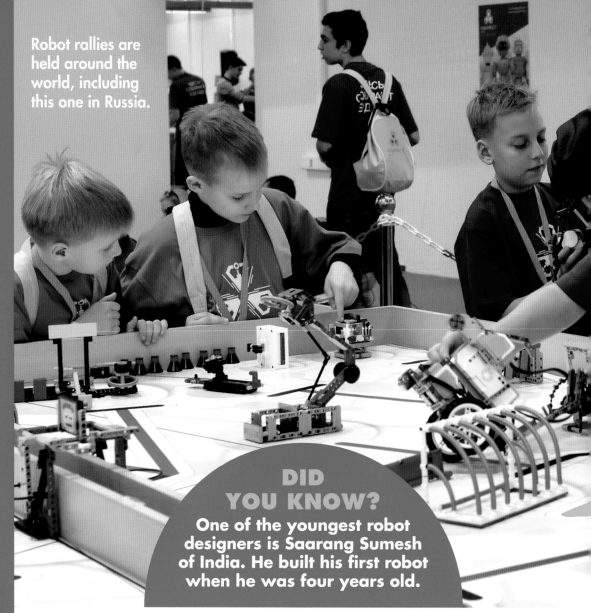

Robot rallies are held around the world, including this one in Russia.

DID YOU KNOW?

One of the youngest robot designers is Saarang Sumesh of India. He built his first robot when he was four years old.

Where can I show off my robot?

At a robot **rally**! Heavy robots push each other off tables. Trucks collect red or blue cubes. Watch one find its way in a maze. Team up with friends. You can build robots that collect trash or help sea turtles. You could win a prize!

CHAPTER TWO

What can robots do?

Anything you build them for! Wheels let them roll. Legs let them walk. Arms pick up and put down. **Sensors** see and hear. A **servo** gives robots life. (Don't forget batteries!) Now type **code** into a tiny computer "brain." It tells the robot how to act.

Tracks let this robot tank roll over rough land.

1. DRAW YOUR ROBOT.

2. BUILD ITS OUTER SHAPE.

3. ATTACH A SERVO.

4. ATTACH A TINY COMPUTER, LIKE A RASPBERRY PI.

5. TYPE IN CODE ON YOUR SMARTPHONE OR TABLET. WATCH YOUR ROBOT GO!

Do robots need me to work?

A boy picks up blocks by using a remote control for a robot arm.

Some robots can do stuff on their own. Just turn them on and watch them go. These robots are **autonomous**. Other robots need your help to do tasks. You move them with a remote control. All robots need to be programmed by humans.

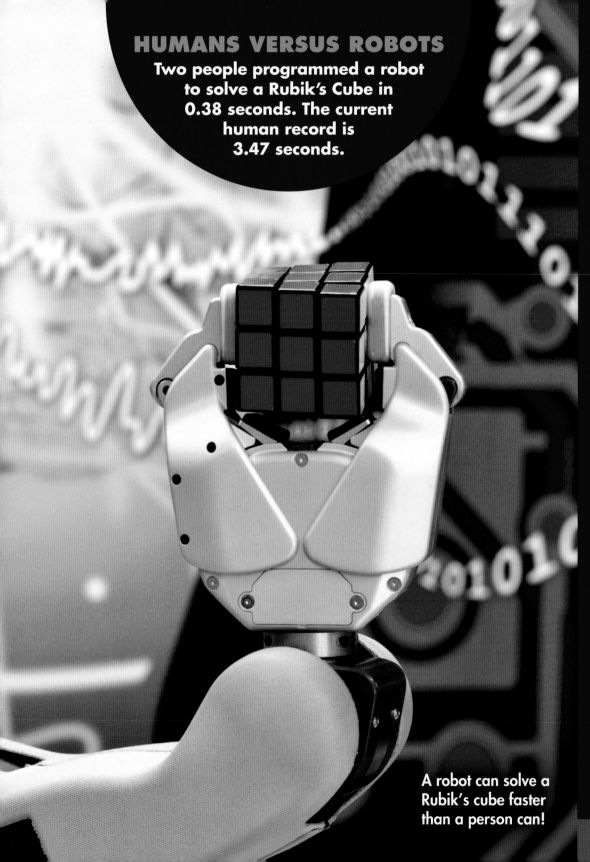

HUMANS VERSUS ROBOTS

Two people programmed a robot to solve a Rubik's Cube in 0.38 seconds. The current human record is 3.47 seconds.

A robot can solve a Rubik's cube faster than a person can!

Robot builders pit their robots against each other in battles.

Can I make robots fight?

BioHazard

Yes! Robots compete in battles. Teams use robots built to crush, spin, or flip other robots. A robot named BioHazard fought on a TV show. It won many times. It threw other robots with its giant arm.

ROBOTS OLD AND NEW

How long have there been robots for kids?

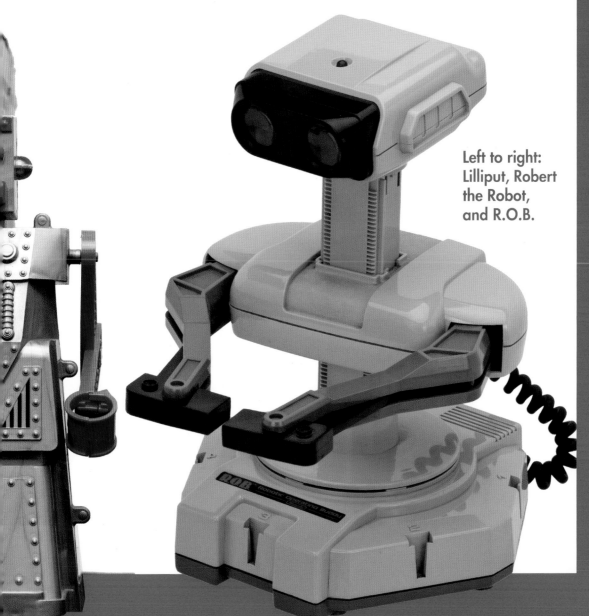

Left to right:
Lilliput, Robert
the Robot,
and R.O.B.

Lilliput was made in Japan in the 1930s. You wound
her up to make her walk. Robert the Robot was
made in 1954. He could talk and walk. His eyes lit
up. R.O.B. came with Nintendo video game systems
in 1985. He pressed buttons and made patterns.

Will robots ever do my homework?

They already can. One robot can copy handwriting. A Chinese schoolgirl used it for her handwriting homework. Two American kids made a robot to solve math homework. It can also write answers in your handwriting. Do you think this is cheating?

A robot arm is programmed to write Chinese characters.

Where can I do LEGO challenges?

You can join a
LEGO robotics team
to learn coding.

Some you can do in your own home. Print out challenges and build them with friends. You can join a LEGO league at school. Work together with your team. Then show off your robot skills at meets around the country!

480,000
That's how many kids, from 110 countries, take part in LEGO robotics challenges around the world.

ASK MORE QUESTIONS

Where can I find a robot club?

What kinds of robots can I build?

Try a BIG QUESTION: How much should we let robots help us?

SEARCH FOR ANSWERS

Search the library catalog or the Internet.
A librarian, teacher, or parent can help you.

Using Keywords
Find the looking glass.

Keywords are the most important words in your question.

?

If you want to know about:

- Finding a robot club, type: FIND ROBOT CLUB KIDS

- Cool robots you can make, type: KIDS MAKE ROBOTS AT HOME

FIND GOOD SOURCES

Are the sources reliable?
Some sources are better than others. An adult can help you. Here are some good, safe sources.

Books
Competition Robots
by Lisa Idzikowski, 2024.

Get Coding with LEGO Mindstorms
by Jenna Vale, 2024.

Internet Sites
Atlanta Hobby Robot Club YouTube Channel
https://www.youtube.com/user/botlanta/videos
Watch and learn as kids compete in robot challenges, from sumo wrestling to cube quests.

Robot Wars Most Destructive Battles
https://www.youtube.com/watch?v=psY_3kOuiRl
Join the action as robots claw, spin, and flip their way to victory!

Every effort has been made to ensure that these websites are appropriate for children. However, because of the nature of the Internet, it is impossible to guarantee that these sites will remain active indefinitely or that their contents will not be altered.

SHARE AND TAKE ACTION

What are some fun tasks for a robot to do at your house?
Could it find your phone? Could it clean your room?

Do you want to learn how to build a DIY robot?
Makerfaire.com has info on upcoming Faires where you can learn to make robots. Check it out here: https://makerfaire.com/upcoming-faires/

Design your own robot.
Make a list of all the boring tasks your robot will do for you. Dishes? Laundry? Making your bed?

GLOSSARY

autonomous Acting on its own without help.

code A set of instructions that humans write into computers.

rally A large meeting for a purpose, such as a competition.

rover A small robot that moves around to explore.

sensor Something that detects light or movement or sound and responds to it.

servo A motor that makes your robot move.

INDEX

About the Author

Lela Nargi is a journalist and the author of 25 science books for kids. She's a long-time sci-fi fan who has always wondered what it would be like to have a useful robot in the house. What tasks would she most want it to do? Making the bed, definitely. For now, she lives in New York City with a dachshund named Bigs who has probably never wondered about robots at all.